THE STORY OF A STR
SABRIN

By
Sheryl Lee

Text Copyright © 2014 Sheryl Lee

To street cats everywhere, but especially Sabrina

TABLE OF CONTENTS

INTRODUCTION
THE BEGINNING
THE NEXT STAGE
NOTHING LASTS FOREVER
SABRINA IS ALONE
THE TURNING POINT
COMES AMADEUS
END NOTES
AFTERWORD

INTRODUCTION

I have already written a short book that features my rescued street cat Sabrina. That book was a book of whimsy, titled *How to Train Your Human*. I wrote it because Sabrina is such a character of a cat, as most of the Egyptian street cats are. However she has suffered a great deal in her short life, and her time before I got her was pretty grim. I don't know what sort of trauma she suffered; I only know the sad physical condition she was in when I got her.

In my time here in Egypt I have observed the street cats, especially those which I feed around my apartment building. There have been territory changes within the cat population, there have been tragedies of small kittens lost or run over by cars. There is one kitten all on her own, she's only a few months old and she looks so sad but I can't get anywhere near her. Sometimes the kittens just disappear and I never know what happened to them. I always hope in those instances that they have been adopted by a caring person unaware that they are in a relatively stable environment.

Some of these street cats are very friendly, some of them will not let me approach and will not eat until I am a safe distance away from them. One mother lost her entire litter, two kittens were run over and two just disappeared. She still has two kittens from a previous litter that depend on her, and of course she will soon come into season, fall pregnant and have another litter of kittens. There is no shortage of cats in Egypt!

There are local people who feed the street cats and seem to be genuinely fond of them. I see the cats coming in and out of their homes so I know that those cats have a place to live whenever they choose. They are still free, they do not belong to these people, they simply choose to visit them and of course to eat the food supplied!

There is a very delicate balance between a sustainable population of cats and over population. The loss of litters of kittens, while very sad, is a natural thing and happens in the wild. Although street cats are technically domestic animals they are mostly wild. They live free, roaming wherever they wish, interacting with all the other street cats and living a very natural life. This means of course a short life for most of them. Disease, accidents and starvation will happen to many, but by no means all of them. I often think that the relationship between the cats and the people caring for them echoes the original relationship Egyptians had with the ancestors of the domestic cat thousands of years ago.

As I said in the beginning, I don't know what happened to Sabrina, why she ended up alone, suffering from malnutrition to the extent that all her bones were showing and her fur was matted and falling out. When she came into my care she was a tiny scrap, too small for her estimated age, with huge eyes shining from a skeletal face and legs too long for her body. She has rewarded me over and over again in the months since with her loving and intuitive nature and highly developed sense of fun and play.

    The following story comes entirely from my imagination. I don't know what happened to her but I can guess from what I have seen and the stories I have been told. This may not be exactly Sabrina's story, but it is the story of many cats and kittens living their lives on the street.

THE BEGINNING

Sabrina's first impressions of life were confusing. There was heat, a multitude of smells, warmth and a moist tongue licking her roughly. Mostly, there was darkness. Over the next several days – a short time for people but a very long time for a cat – she gradually learned to sift through the bewildering array of impressions to build a cohesive picture of her surroundings.

She had a mother; she smelled of milk and was always warm and soft. She had siblings, three of them who spent a lot of time lying in a heap with her and competing with her for the best milk nipple to latch onto. Her first few days were warm, dark, safe and quiet.

Over the next few days her eyes began to open and she adjusted to the sense of sight opening up the world for her. At first her vision was fuzzy, she could see shapes and colours but not much detail. Gradually her vision cleared and she could see her siblings, her mother and her surroundings. Her siblings were black and white, ginger and white and tortoiseshell. Not that she knew the colours or saw them very clearly but a human would have named them so. She didn't know what she looked like and didn't care. She was however the standout among them, being almost entirely white with tortoiseshell markings on her head and her tail, like a Turkish Van cat. Her mother was tortoiseshell, a very pretty blend of colours with beautiful glass green eyes.

They lived among the broken bricks that were piled up underneath the first floor of an incomplete apartment building. There were no humans around this area, and they were beside the very back wall deep in the shadows and well hidden from view. Their mother had chosen their hiding spot well.

After some more time had passed Sabrina and her siblings were able to walk and run, and their ears had opened up so that they could hear. They became more adventurous, exploring their immediate surroundings and playing among the bricks and other building detritus left behind when the building was abandoned. There were other cats around and often their mother would become involved in a dispute over ownership of their area. She was always triumphant with no actual fighting taking place, reinforcing Sabrina's impression of the world as a safe place.

Sabrina saw people walking past, and often saw them stop to pat her mother. Sometimes they would bring food, which her mother always brought back to share with her kittens. Sabrina was very curious about people, but not yet brave enough to get closer. As the kittens got older and stronger their mother left them for longer periods of time while she hunted for food. Sometimes she brought back a rat or a mouse, sometimes it was meat she had foraged from a bin or rubbish bag and sometimes it was the food people left for them.

Sabrina and her siblings ate whatever their mother brought to them, they were always hungry as they were growing very fast and their mother's milk was no longer enough to sustain them fully. One day their mother was away for a very long time and Sabrina and her siblings became bored. They started running and chasing each other, tumbling over each other and leaping high in the air. Without noticing they moved ever closer to the sunlight at the front of their building and to the outside world.

The bright rays of the sun shining into her eyes alerted Sabrina to their position. Her siblings ran back several feet in panic, but she stayed where she was. The sun was warm on her fur and it was an enjoyable feeling. She blinked as her eyes adjusted to a much brighter light than they were used to, and she looked around at a world far bigger than she had seen before in her short life. She could see people walking but none were close to them so she dismissed them from her mind and focused on the many other strange sights.

There were a couple of parked cars, a large flowering bougainvillea, two metal rubbish bins overflowing with bags and boxes, plus several other cats in her immediate vicinity. Sabrina froze when she saw them, but the other cats seemed non-threatening and she relaxed again. Her black and white brother crept forward to stand with her and she bumped heads with him in a gesture of reassurance – a gesture that made both of them feel better.

Sabrina felt safe enough to sit down and observe her suddenly much larger horizon, only running back to safety when a couple of people approached with hands extended in greeting. She and her brother both ran back to their familiar home in a panic, but Sabrina crept forward just a bit again, to see if the people were still there. They were not – she was not sure if she was happy or sad about this.

THE NEXT STAGE

As the kittens grew their mother spent more and more time away from them and they in turn became more adventurous. Sabrina spent a lot of time sitting at the very front of the abandoned building watching the world outside her territory. Some of the other cats would greet her gently and she was no longer afraid of them. People still tried to be friendly but she always ran back under their roof if people got too close to her. Her siblings joined her sometimes, especially her black and white brother, but they did not share her fascination.

Every day the same two people walked past and spoke to her. When she ran from them the first time they didn't try to approach her again, just greeted her as they walked by. One day they brought some chicken meat and dropped it in front of her. She ate it as fast as she could, knowing that her siblings would smell the food and come running. She sniffed the finger of one of the people, it smelled like chicken and something else which she assumed was a human smell. It was strange but not a bad smell.

When her siblings smelled the food and rushed forward there was not much left. Sabrina stepped back so they could have the remains. The people watched them eat and then left but they were back the next day with more food. This time her siblings came straight away, but the people had brought enough food for them all. After that the people came every day with food. Sabrina and her siblings began to wait for them and a friendship formed between them all. Sabrina and her siblings would let the people pat them, and they would eat the food gratefully. They began to feel less hungry all the time, and stronger. The people brought food for the other cats around too, so there was no fighting among them.

Their mother was there one day and she ate the food so fast the people left and came back in a short time with more for their mother. After that their mother waited with them for the food. Sabrina and her siblings noticed there was more milk for them, and they were happy their mother spent more time with them. It was a very good time in Sabrina's life, which until then had been relatively uneventful.

The days passed, the kittens grew bigger and stronger while their mother grew sleeker and more beautiful. The cats around them were happier and there was peace in their little area of the town. The people continued to come every day and seemed happy to just pat them while they ate. Sabrina was curious about where they went and one day she followed them a short distance. But when they reached unfamiliar territory she became afraid and ran back to her home.

Each day the people came with food and each day Sabrina followed them a little further. They seemed to like it but they didn't encourage her. She never went far enough to lose sight of her home, she was just curious. Sometimes her black and white brother came with her a little way, but he always turned back before she did.

As the kittens grew bigger they ate more food and drank less from their mother, but they still relied on her milk and they still slept with her. Even though their mother spent a lot of time away from them she was always with them at night to protect them.

The people brought larger quantities of food as the kittens grew and they also ate the food their mother brought to them. They had begun exploring the bins outside their building and sometimes found food there as well. They were not fussy, they ate anything they found. They ate the mixture of soaked dry food, rice and meat that the people brought, the bits of meat and bones and bread their mother brought, the occasional rat or mouse, and various left over foods found in the bins. They preferred the food the people brought but they were street cats – they were born into a life where the food supply was erratic and any and all food was to be eaten.

NOTHING LASTS FOREVER

The day when it all changed began like any other. Sabrina and her siblings played in the morning sunshine while their mother went off searching for food. But on this day men came, and machines, and trucks. The abandoned building was about to be finished and the kittens' home was no longer safe. The kittens didn't know this of course. Bewildered they ran to the bins across the road and hid behind them as the men began to work on the building again.

Building supplies, sand and cement were unloaded and piled in front of the building. There was so much movement and noise from the machines and the men that the kittens were too afraid to move from their hiding spot. They wanted their mother but she was far away and unaware of what was happening. They huddled together and watched and listened, and waited for their mother to come.

The hours passed and still the kittens stayed hidden. Their people came and stopped in shock to see the work going on at the building. They looked around for the kittens but the kittens were so afraid that they didn't come out from behind the bins. The people searched around the building but they didn't think to look behind the bins. Eventually they moved on and Sabrina watched them go with sadness.

Work stopped and there was silence. After a while Sabrina became brave enough to peep out from behind the bins, but the men were still there, they were eating. As she watched one of them got up and came to the bins to throw in his rubbish. That was when he saw the kittens. But he didn't talk softly to them and he didn't offer them food. Instead he shouted in a loud and frightening voice and kicked at them.

Sabrina and her siblings were terrified and ran. They ran together, searching for a hiding place and the man chased them, shouting and laughing. They scurried through a hole in a wall and rushed to a bush where they piled together, eyes huge in their faces. But this was the yard of a villa that had a dog and that dog did not want kittens. It barked and growled at them and they rushed to the hole in the wall again, squeezing out as fast as they could. Sabrina was last and she felt a sharp pain in her tail where the dog bit, trying to get to her.

Outside they were thankful to see that the man was no longer around. They looked back towards their home, but were too frightened to go back yet. Seeing a large bougainvillea against a wall Sabrina led her siblings to that. They squeezed in between the branches until they were pressed up against the wall and there they stayed all afternoon. Traumatised, afraid to come out they eventually slept huddled together. They were scared, hungry and thirsty but they didn't move from their spot until it was dark.

Once it was dark and quiet they ventured out, and crept back towards their home. They expected to see their mother there, but she wasn't. They searched and called for her but she didn't come. Hungry, they foraged in the bins for food and found some discarded bread and a few pieces of meat. They were thirsty too, but their mother was not there. Sabrina knew they couldn't stay at the bins, the men would come back the next day. But this was the only place they knew, and the only place their mother would come looking for them. So they stayed there waiting, but their mother still did not come.

At dawn they left the bins, too afraid to stay any longer. They wandered the back streets, looking for their mother or for anyone that would help them. But they didn't find their mother, and they never saw her again. That day the kittens found a new hiding place a short distance from their old home. It was another empty building and there were already cats living there, but they accepted the arrival of the kittens without complaint.

They never saw the people who had fed them again either, and without their mother they had to find all of their own food. They were too young to look after themselves but they managed to find enough food to survive, and to get water every now and then when shop owners hosed down the front of their stores.

The days passed and the kittens began to grow used to this frightening new life. They still called for their mother every night but she never came and after a week they stopped calling. Life settled into a new pattern of constantly searching for food. The kittens slept together, grooming each other for comfort. They still played together - they were still very young - but they spent more time searching for food and quickly grew thinner without their mother's milk and the regular food from their people.

SABRINA IS ALONE

One day some people came and saw the kittens sleeping huddled together. These people had no empathy or understanding of small and helpless creatures. They thought it would be fun to throw stones at the kittens and each gathered up a handful. The kittens were woken by stones pelting into their soft skin. Panicked they ran, and the people chased them, laughing and still throwing the stones.

For the first time in their lives the kittens became separated as they tried to get away from the stones and the people. They were running for their lives because the foolish people had no understanding of how easy it is to kill a small kitten. Sabrina did not know where her siblings went, they were all so panicked that they just ran.

Her siblings all found narrow spaces in which to hide, and eventually Sabrina did too. Safe for the time being she tucked herself into the space between some large cement pipes she had crawled into and stared out to see if the people were still after her. They were not, they had run out of stones and were walking away laughing about the fun they had just had. They did not think about what they had done, about the devastation they had just wreaked on four tiny little creatures. They forgot about the kittens altogether.

But the kittens were now separated and had to try to find each other again. Alone for the first time in their lives they all stayed in the places they had hidden, too afraid to come out. Eventually they did, trying to find their way back to the building they were living in. The three siblings found their way back, but Sabrina did not. When she came out from her hiding place she was spotted by a small child who was excited to see her and squealed. The child was being friendly; she wanted to pat Sabrina and in fact had Sabrina not run again she may well have found a home with the child's family.

However Sabrina was still traumatised by what had happened and when the child squealed she panicked and ran again. By the time she stopped she was completely lost. Now Sabrina was alone, in a strange part of the town and lost. She never found her way back to the building and she never saw her siblings again.

It was a very hard time for Sabrina. She had never been alone, had never slept alone or eaten alone. Some of the cats she saw were friendly, and some chased her away. She foraged for food, digging through plastic bags and rubbish bins and eating anything she could find. She grew thinner by the day, and her fur began to lose its shine. Her gleaming white coat became a dirty grey colour, and the fur on the bottom of her feet became matted and clumped.

She learned to stay away from cars that were moving or had their engines running, and she learned that shop keepers would most often chase her away although some didn't. She never forgot her experience with the dog and hid every time she saw one. Some of the people she approached were kind and gave her food – one person gave her a can of sardines which was the best meal she had enjoyed in a very long time. But she didn't stay in one place, she kept moving. She was searching, constantly searching for her siblings and her mother.

She learned very quickly to be wary of people. A few times she was chased and had stones thrown at her, experiences which brought back the day she lost her siblings and which consequently terrified her. One time a man crept up to her where she was sleeping and hit her with a stick. It hit her on the front leg and she woke in a panic and ran. When she found a dark hiding place between some large pieces of broken cement she stayed and rested, licking her sore leg. She limped for several days after that and never lost a fear of sudden movement from people, or of loud noises.

However Sabrina had a well-developed sense of intuition which was swiftly honed by her experiences in the street. She was also very intelligent and soon learned to read the body language and the tone of voice of the people she saw. She learned to sense which people were safe to approach and which to avoid and after that was not kicked or hit nearly as often. She stayed on the move, still trying to find her family.

THE TURNING POINT

The change came one day when Sabrina saw a woman who looked like one of the people who used to feed her and her family. She approached this woman who picked her up, felt her bones and her fur and took her back to her apartment. Sabrina had never been inside an apartment before, but she didn't worry about it because the woman gave her cooked chicken breast and she was a very hungry, having found very little food over the last few days.

It was the best meal Sabrina had ever had. She found the door closed after she had eaten, but the door to the courtyard was open so she went out that door and explored her new surroundings. The woman put down a container filled with sand, which Sabrina instantly understood was to be a toilet for her. She was grateful for this as she was a very clean cat even in her current circumstances. She used the tray and then went back inside the apartment. Inside the woman put down a bowl of water which Sabrina sniffed at before drinking. She felt so much better after eating and drinking that she sat down in the middle of the room and tried to clean herself.

The woman picked her up and sat with Sabrina in her lap. It was a very unfamiliar feeling, but Sabrina had not felt the touch of any other creature in a long time and she missed the feel of her siblings and her mother. So she stayed in the woman's lap and allowed her to pat her. If felt good, so good that Sabrina began to purr and in a very short time had fallen asleep.

After that Sabrina decided to stay with the woman for a while. She was starved in more ways than one. She was physically starved and ate anything that the woman gave her with gratitude. She drank water, used the litter tray and tried to clean her fur. But she was also emotionally starved. She was a kitten who had lost her mother and then her siblings. She had been chased, hit, kicked and frightened. She had spent a long time alone when she should have been with a family. She was starved of affection and took every opportunity to sit in the woman's lap, needing the comfort of touch as much as she needed food.

One day another woman came to visit. She brought a strange bag with her and put it on the floor. Sabrina ran in from the courtyard when she heard this woman's voice. It was the language of the people who had fed her and her family so long ago. This new woman picked her up and Sabrina stared into her eyes. Whatever she saw there satisfied her and she put her front paws around the woman's neck and held on tightly. The woman sat with her in her lap, and then after a short time both women took Sabrina into the bathroom where she had her first bath.

It was not an experience Sabrina enjoyed, although she was not frightened. But like most cats she hated getting wet. However when it was done and she was dried she realised she felt much better. She was clean, and the matted fur on her back legs and under her front feet was gone. She shook herself, and then sat down in the new woman's lap and cleaned and dried herself.

When the woman put her in the strange bag and took her to another apartment Sabrina did not complain. She knew that this was to be her person, the one she would stay with from now on. At this new apartment Sabrina was given a lot of food that came from a packet, along with cooked chicken and dry food. Those first few weeks she ate and ate, she couldn't get full. She couldn't get enough of touch either, and sat in this new person's lap as often as she could or rode on her shoulder when she could not.

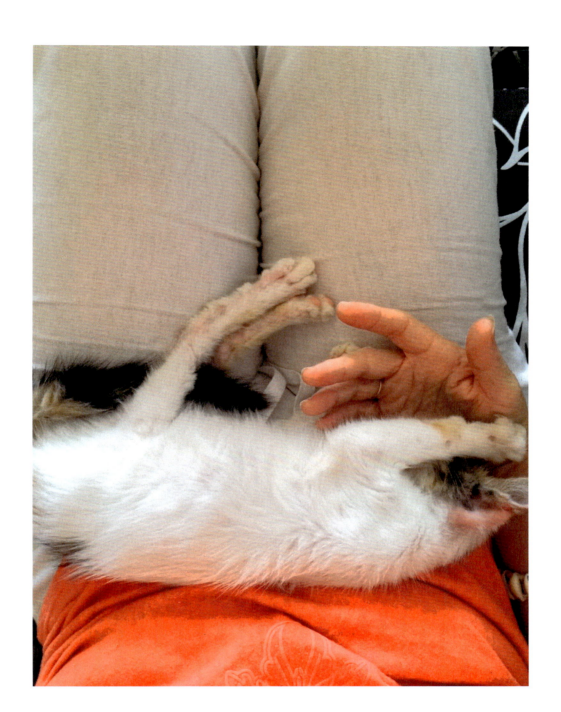

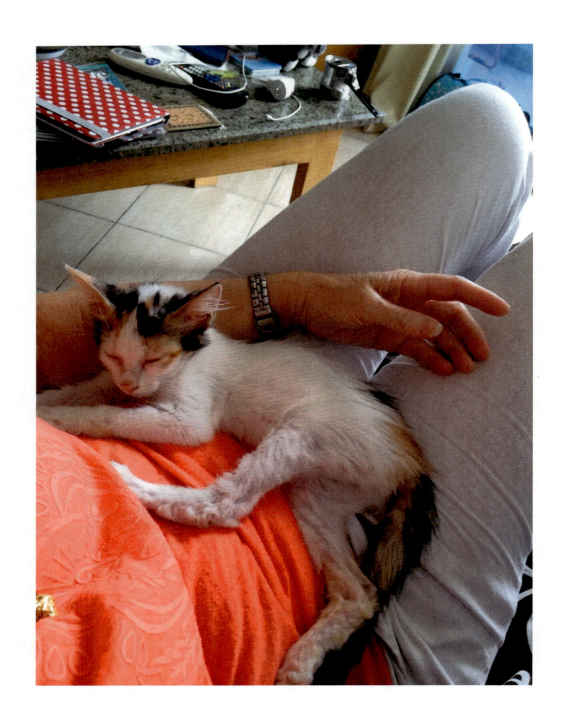

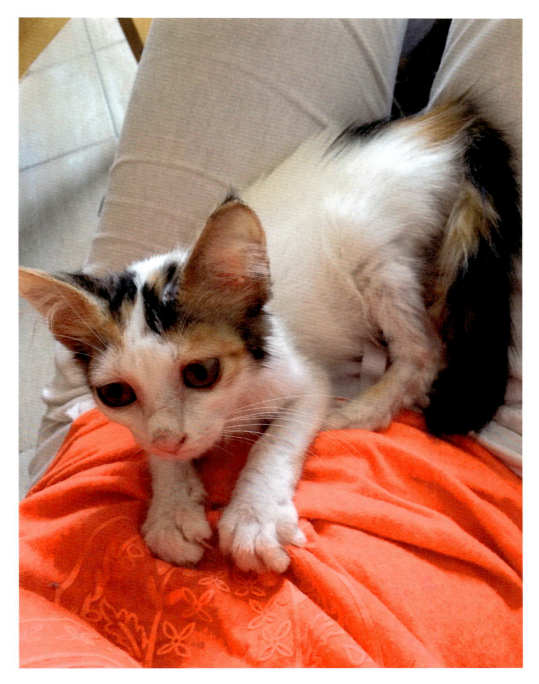

    She spent a lot of time in those weeks staring out of the glass door to the balcony, wondering where her family was and if her siblings were ok. She missed her family; street cats have extended families and if she, her siblings and their mother had not been separated they would have stayed together even after her mother had more kittens. As much as she loved her new person, she was lonely.

    Her physical condition improved quickly however. Her coat began to grow back on her legs and behind her ears, and began to get thick and develop a shine again. She started to put on weight and in a few weeks did not look so much like a walking skeleton. Her eyes remained huge in her face, they were a luminous green that was quite beautiful. Her face filled out, looking rounder and less pointed although no less elegant. But still, she was lonely.

COMES AMADEUS

Then one day another kitten came to the apartment. He was a tiny grey and white ball of fluff. Sabrina, on seeing him, forgot that she was lonely and became instead indignant that another cat had invaded her space.

The kitten, which was named Amadeus, did not much care what she thought; he was too busy being afraid and lonely himself. He cried for days, a sound that was intensely annoying to Sabrina although her human seemed very patient with it. But in time the crying stopped and he became playful. Sabrina watched, still annoyed that she now had to share her person with this kitten.

After a few days however she found herself curious about this little creature and began to play with him. He at first reacted with fear, understandable since she had refused to have anything to do with him for several days. But after a while he accepted her overtures and they played for some time. They still slept separately but Sabrina found herself quite enjoying his company.

One day after they played she stayed with him and began to clean his ears. He wriggled and squirmed, like her black and white sibling used to do. She held him down as she did with her sibling and continued to clean him. It was the beginning of their bonding. A few weeks later Sabrina and Amadeus were bonded as strongly as Sabrina had been bonded to her siblings, and most likely Amadeus to his.

Now Sabrina and Amadeus are inseparable. The tiny little grey and white ball of fluff has grown much bigger than Sabrina, who has remained a small and delicate cat. However she is still very much the boss in the relationship. They play together, groom together, sleep together, eat together. They lie entwined with each other as they would have done with their siblings if they had still been with their families.

Although they lost their families, they were lucky because they found a home and they found each other. Neither are lonely anymore and it's a wonderful thing to see.

    I don't know what happened to Sabrina's family, she was found alone in the street on the verge of starvation. Amadeus was rescued before he lost much condition although he had also lost his mother. He was a fat little butterball and the only indication of his eventual size was the great big feet he was always tripping over like a clumsy puppy. Amadeus is such a soft and gentle little soul that I fear he would have fared even worse than Sabrina had he been left alone for much longer. And he was a baby whereas she was a couple of months old.

    They are two of the happy ending stories of the street cats. There are many more, stories of rescued cats and stories of the cats living on the streets that have found people to take care of them. There are also heartbreaking stories of the ones that didn't make it and weren't lucky. It is the flow of life.

END NOTES

Both of my cats have a story to tell, and Sabrina's would be the longest and most harrowing. Possibly worse things happened to her than I recounted. It is quite likely that her mother and her siblings were killed, but even writing her story as a piece of fiction I couldn't bring myself to introduce that much trauma. For whatever reason, she was alone and she was not coping well with it as she was just too young to fend for herself.

That she still approached the woman who found her tells a great deal about her capacity for love. This kitten was treated very badly and had no reason to trust people, and yet she still gave unstinting friendship to the woman who found her, and unconditional love to me. With me she has never shown any fear except that sudden loud noises and sudden movement frighten her and she becomes distressed at any but the most gentle of handling.

She is, as are most cats I think, a blend of fragility and strength. Perhaps this is part of the charm of cats, this fragile exterior, but with intelligence far in excess of their size. Sabrina has become the most loving and loyal cat I have ever owned. She is funny, charming and sweet and she plays the cute card brilliantly whenever she wants something!

When I first got her she would routinely steal food off my plate when I was not looking, including the local bread which she would take under the coffee table and tear apart, eating with apparent relish. However these days she is a very pampered creature and considers herself far too good for bread. She turns up her nose at the food I prepare for the street cats as well, although occasionally she will steal part of it, perhaps to remind herself of her origins.

AFTERWORD

I wish I could save all of the cats I find, but I have limited capacity in terms of space and also finances. The local shelters have the same problem of course, and so I do what I can by feeding the cats around me. It can be very rewarding but also sad, such as when cats I am feeding stop coming and I wonder what happened to them, or when kittens are killed or simply disappear.

There are people who help the cats, and those who would kill them which I think is the same anywhere in the world. There are dangers in the form of the street dogs, people and cars. There is the possibility of disease, accidents and starvation if a kitten is alone too young.

But in this climate, in this country, the cats can live a happy life. The weather is very hot in summer, but these cats are descendants of the African Wild Cat; they can handle the heat if they have access to water. It is never very cold so winters are quite comfortable for them. There are many cars on the main roads but the back streets are much quieter and there are many buildings in various stages of construction plus many abandoned buildings which make good homes for families of cats.

One thing I have observed is that the cats have extended families, much like prides of wild cats such as lions. One mother may be living with two or three litters of kittens, and the tomcats are living in close proximity as well. Several families seem able to co-exist, sisters will raise their kittens together. Clearly there is safety in numbers and the cats seem to realise this. I have also noticed that even the tomcats are gentle animals. All of the street cats are basically gentle, friendly creatures. Some are wilder than others but I have not seen any that are hostile.

There is a small tortoiseshell cat living up the road behind my apartment building who seems to be the queen of the area. She is the one who lost her current litter one by one, but still has two kittens from a previous litter living with her. She goes with me when I feed all of the cats, and she approaches every strange cat she sees. Some she allows and some she chases off.

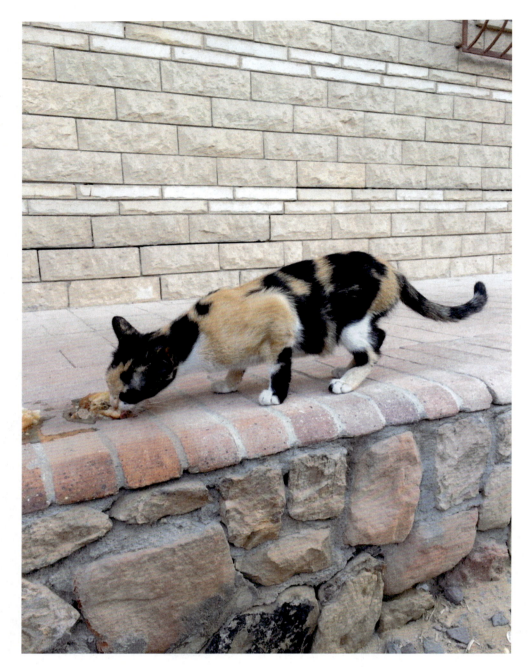

    The dominant tomcat is a large black and white fellow who rules this area over the other tomcats. He is not aggressive though, I haven't seen him fight although I daresay he does when necessary. He is gentle with the kittens, allowing them to push him away and eat his food but he will not tolerate that from a full grown male cat. He has the sweetest expression on his face and is very wary of people. I have no doubt he is chased often since he is a tomcat and they can be rather unpleasant to have around with their tendency to pee on everything.

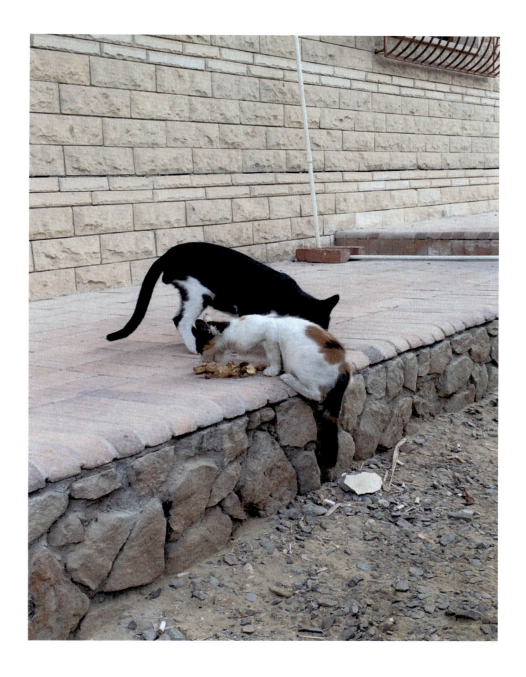

    I expect he is the father of most of the kittens around here. Certainly two of the lost kittens were black and white. Of the other kittens, there is a litter of five, all ginger tabby in colour except for a traditional mau coloured one. Their mother is also a traditional mau. There is another litter comprising three kittens, one a pale ginger mau, one a calico and one ginger and white. Their mother is sister to the other and is ginger and white. There is also the little lost kitten, she is a female calico and is very timid. She wants to be part of the family but the tortoiseshell queen while tolerating her presence will not allow her to get close. That is her pictured above with the tomcat which is letting her eat from his food.

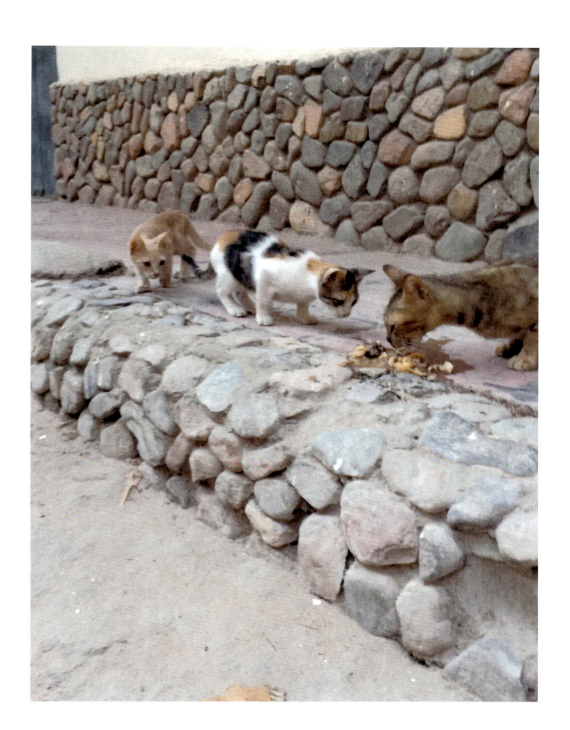

    The only real way to ensure that the balance of the population remains stable and sustainable is to neuter the street cats, not all of them, but as many of them as is possible. The less breeding numbers there are the slower the population growth. As well as being fed by many residents of the towns and cities of Egypt (specifically Hurghaga as that is where I am living and where I can observe first-hand what is happening with the cats) the street cats live quite well on the rubbish left out in the streets. In Hurghada and I believe in most of the towns of Egypt there are many bags of rubbish piled up in parts of the back streets. The cats – and the street dogs of which there are many as well – can forage in the rubbish for food. If the population is regulated by consistent neutering there would be plenty of food available for the street cats, and the street dogs also. That is the goal of the local animal shelters here, as it is in other parts of Egypt and in the rest of the world too where there is a street cat problem.

The cats perform a vital task in that they keep down the numbers of vermin, as they have been doing for thousands of years. In the middle ages when persecution of cats was high – when they were considered familiars of witches and destroyed in the thousands –the cat population was so devastated that the balance between cats and vermin was lost and rats and mice thrived. This was followed by the black plague, spread by rats which were no longer controlled by the cats.

So the street cats perform a very important task of keeping down the numbers of vermin which would otherwise enjoy something of a population explosion. I don't know about you, but when out walking I am much happier greeting a friendly cat than being bitten by a non-friendly rat!

I hope you enjoyed this little book. I really love writing these short reads and taking and selecting the photos for inclusion. If you liked this one please go and check out my others. And then go pat you cat!

Made in the USA
Middletown, DE
25 November 2016